PET GROOMING IS LIKE MOUNTAIN CLIMBING

How to Overcome Your Hugest Obstacles

Tanya Ellis

Co-authored with Raymond Aaron

AuthoritiesPress

PET GROOMING IS LIKE MOUNTAIN CLIMBING:
How to Overcome Your Hugest Obstacles
www.tanyaellis.com
Copyright © 2022 Tanya Ellis

Paperback ISBN: 978-1-77277-520-4

All rights reserved. No portion of this book may be reproduced mechanically, electronically, or by any other means, including photocopying, without permission of the publisher or author except in the case of brief quotations embodied in critical articles and reviews. It is illegal to copy this book, post it to a website, or distribute it by any other means without permission from the publisher or author.

References to internet websites (URLs) were accurate at the time of writing. Authors and the publishers are not responsible for URLs that may have expired or changed since the manuscript was prepared.

Limits of Liability and Disclaimer of Warranty
The author and publisher shall not be liable for your misuse of the enclosed material. This book is strictly for informational and educational purposes only.

Warning – Disclaimer
The purpose of this book is to educate and entertain. The author and/or publisher do not guarantee that anyone following these techniques, suggestions, tips, ideas, or strategies will become successful. The author and/or publisher shall have neither liability nor responsibility to anyone with respect to any loss or damage caused, or alleged to be caused, directly or indirectly by the information contained in this book.

Publisher
10-10-10 Publishing
Markham, ON Canada

Printed in Canada and the United States of America

To all my clients, past and present, thank you for allowing me to care for your furry family members. It has been an honor to be a part of your lives.

Table of Contents

Acknowledgments vii
Foreword ix

Chapter 1: The View From the Top of the Mountain ...1
Taking Another Leap 7
Understanding the Potential Risk.................................10
Mental Toughness to Keep Going 12

Chapter 2: Packing Your Backpack For Business 15
Take Practice Steps to Manage Your Initial Investment 19
Setting the Goals for Your Business 20
Is Your Backpack Ready? 21
Get Inspired by Others 24
Pick a Passion...25

Chapter 3: Building a Solid Foundation 27
Finding the Right Guide 29
Changing Your Mentality 31
What You Don't Know Can Slow You Down 33

Chapter 4: Setting Goals to Reach the Summit........39
Setting Goals for Success...41
Define the Journey With a Business Plan 44
Remember the Importance of a Network 47

Chapter 5: Have You Hit the Wall? 51
Imagination 54
Be Able to Pivot 55
Delegate for Growth 57
Innovate to Build the Next Stage 58
Create Consistent Lines of Communication 59
Being Proactive to Keep Your Team Running Smoothly 61

Chapter 6: Growth is Never-Ending 63
Your Dreams Are the Goals 66
Be Aware of Blind Spots 67
Do You Have Goals or Objectives? 68
Align Your Goals to Your Vision for Growth 72

Chapter 7: Running a Business in Challenging Times 75
Define the Problem or the Damage 77
Controlling Your Response 79
Focus on Your Long-Term Business Goals 80
Communicate the Challenge to Your Team 81
Collaborate on a Solution 82
Are You Aware of the Situation? 83

Chapter 8: You Reached the Summit – Now What? .. 87
Planning for the Future by Defining Your Niche 89
Making the Decision to Exit 91
What Exit Strategy Works for You? 94

Chapter 9: Building on Your Passion for Pets 101
The Benefits of Coaching 104
Beyond the Exit 108

Chapter 10: Start Climbing to Your Summit! 113
Lessons From a Pet Groomer 116
Reaching the Summit 119
Growth is a Mindset 121

About the Author 125

Acknowledgments

First, I want to say thank you to all those individuals who have supported me over the years. There are too many to mention here, but the list includes family, friends, and mentors. I simply could not have accomplished all that I did without you all!

I want to acknowledge my team Pooches N' Pals, Pooches N' The Bluffs, and The Dog House, past and present. If it weren't for them, I wouldn't be where I am today! This team is so incredible. They work their tails off to make sure that they care for dogs the same way I would!

Foreword

Pet grooming entrepreneur Tanya Ellis is passionate about teaching you how to successfully run your own pet grooming business. In *Pet Grooming Is Like Mountain Climbing: How to Overcome Your Hugest Obstacles*, Tanya shares her personal experiences as both a business owner and a mountain climber.

With a sense of humor and years of experience, Tanya teaches you how to avoid potential pitfalls that could limit the success of your business. She also shares how creativity and unconventional marketing ideas can spread the word to others about your business and what you offer. *Pet Grooming Is Like Mountain Climbing* is a true guidebook that steps outside of traditional business books by sharing the author's real-life experiences in the pet industry.

Tanya also shares how a challenging situation, like climbing a mountain, can teach you skills necessary to run a successful business. Not only is she imparting critical knowledge on practical items, like managing costs, but she also talks about the long-term plan for your business, and how to create a viable and strategic business plan.

For bonuses go to www.poochesandpalsinc.com

Pet Grooming Is Like Mountain Climbing: How to Overcome Your Hugest Obstacles is an inspiring look into the world of pet grooming, giving you the benefit of experience and practical tools to grow your business successfully.

Loral Langemeier
The Millionaire Maker

Chapter 1

The View From the Top of the Mountain

It was breathtaking! As I stood at the top of Mount Kilimanjaro, I could see for miles around. I felt as if I had been lifted above all the noise of the world. Reaching the top had given me a new perspective on life, and it was an exhilarating experience. How did I get to the top, and what made me decide to take this journey?

To be honest, I had never been interested in climbing a mountain. When I was a little girl, my dream was to go to Africa. I read all the books and learned about different animals. Going on safari was on my bucket list. In 2009, a friend reached out to me. She was part of a group that was going to climb Mount Kilimanjaro and, since I had wanted to go to Africa, she asked if I wanted to join the group from the Multiple Sclerosis (MS) Society of Canada that would be taking the trip.

As a part of this group, each participant needed to raise $10,000. What was the connection between mountain climbing and MS? Well, individuals who are diagnosed with MS often have symptoms that are similar to mountain sickness. It sounded like a really great cause and, even though I never thought about climbing a mountain, I decided to go for it.

For bonuses go to ...

Plus, the trip included a safari. For me, it was a win-win, and I was doing something I never thought about doing; something I had always dreamed of doing.

I remember the day we left. After reaching the airport and getting through security, we boarded the plane. I originally had to sit in the middle seat. Now if you have ever traveled anywhere longer than a couple of hours on a plane, you know how uncomfortable it can be. A couple boarded and asked if I preferred to sit in the middle. I said no, so they got to sit together, and I got a window seat. It was a win-win. When I transferred planes later in the trip, I ended up with an aisle seat. "I can already tell this will be the best trip," I wrote in my journal. My excitement grew as we flew over Egypt. I even noted in my journal what time we would arrive.

After meeting our mountain guide, Julius, we soon left the airport and headed to our destination, the L'Oasis Lodge. It was a cute and small place, with huts and really friendly people. We were about 450 feet above sea level, and that meant everyone was drinking a lot of water to stay hydrated. After relaxing and exploring the area around the lodge, we had a couple of meetings, one of which was about the climb that we would begin on Sunday.

After a long four-hour drive from the lodge to the base of the mountain on Sunday, we were introduced to the porters. Julius led us onto the beginning of the climb. We were at 2500 feet above sea level. It was not easy, and the weather was warm enough to wear a t-shirt for the first couple days of the climb. On the second day of our climb, I woke up, got ready for the day, and gathered my things before heading to the mess tent where I could get breakfast. That warm porridge, eggs, and sausage hit the spot. I had hardly been able to sleep the night before, which I think was because I was overtired. Over the course of our second day of climbing, we trekked for six hours, taking frequent breaks, and resting when necessary.

One of the members of our group ended up going back down when we stopped for lunch because she was feeling sick. At lunch, I was journaling and noted that we were halfway to our next camp. As I was listening to some tunes and walking up the trail, I started thinking about how I could be a better person, what I could do better, how I treat others, and how I treat myself. I realized that I am just as worthy as anyone else. The problem is that I, like most of us, didn't believe that.

I also found a stick that looked like a finger pointing toward the summit. At the end of that day's walk, I decided to start walking with a pole, as I had come close to twisting my ankle several times.

The next stage of the climb was steeper than previously. There were snowstorms and the weather began to shift from comfortable to colder. As we walked up, it just kept getting colder and colder. The porter that I was walking with ended up being my guide that day. He offered me warm water during the climb, which I appreciated as the temperature dropped.

We talked a lot, getting to know each other. It was a long diagonal zigzag walk all the way up on the last day, and we started climbing at midnight, so it was pitch dark and all we had were flashlights to see in front of us. Something cool, though, was that someone had a boom

For bonuses go to ...

box and was playing Bob Marley, which kept me motivated as well. We reached Gillman's Point, and I said I couldn't go any further. My guide kept encouraging me to keep going. Eventually, we reached the summit. The view was breathtaking and, after I looked around, I realized that I just wanted to get down. My head was pounding because I had a massive headache.

The climb down was more grueling in many ways because I was tired, and my head hurt. Others in the group were not feeling well. In fact, one guy had to be carried down. I also had some help from 2 porters who held both of my arms, and ran me down the scree quickly, to a more flat part. I walked the rest of the way down to camp for a short nap before we had to leave again to go back down, so the next group of climbers could set up camp. But after days of struggling to get a good night's sleep, I slept like a baby during that nap. The rest of the climb down was tiring, but I was proud of myself when I got to the bottom. We enjoyed a super fun celebration with the porters and guides, and we danced and clapped and enjoyed our accomplishment. I believe we should take time to celebrate our accomplishments regularly.

We also went to the gates to get our certificates. Those of us who made it to the very top received a certificate stating that we finished the climb to 5895 meters above sea level, or 19340 feet. After that we had a chance to thank our porters and the staff for helping us make it, tip them and give away the things we no longer needed or wanted. I gave away some clothing, my MP3 player, and a few other things that could help them out. We headed back to L'Oasis, where I was able to shower and get cleaned up.

The whole journey was incredible and taught me a lot about myself, while exposing me to other peoples and cultures. It also served as an inspiration for what I ended up doing in the future as an entrepreneur.

Taking Another Leap

Years later, I bought a business. In many ways, that business was also a mountain that needed to be climbed. There are many connections between that first mountain trip and starting my business. I hadn't been sure that I wanted to own a business but, like the mountain trip, when the opportunity presented itself, I took the leap.

Perhaps you have been working in your industry for years. You might enjoy what you do, but you have a sense that you could be achieving so much more. Maybe you never thought of owning a business, much like I never thought about climbing a mountain. Throughout this book, my goal is to show you the journey of going up a mountain, and how similar it is to starting and owning a business, be it in pet grooming or some other industry.

My goal is to get you excited about what is possible. Too often, we get attached to a paycheck, never stopping to think about whether the job we are doing is fulfilling our passion or helping us to reach our goals. Instead, we fall into the routine of life. Years go by. At some point, we look up and realize that we are nowhere near our dream life. Instead, we are stuck in a job we don't like.

The beauty of life is that we can change course. It is possible to start from right now, achieve the career that you want, and own the business that will help to make your dreams possible.

With a little luck, hard work, and a willingness to take a risk, you can achieve incredible things, including climbing a mountain. However, before I could take off and climb that mountain, I had to do some prep work. First, there was the fundraising, so I could even be included on the trip. I also had to start preparing physically for the demands that climbing were going to make on my body.

In the world of business, there is a lot of prep work before we can dive into owning a business. That could include learning about the industry, understanding where there might be an opportunity to capture a portion of the market. What can you offer that no one else is currently offering?

I love animals and always have. I was a dog lover, even as a child. My parents didn't want us to get a dog because of the responsibility that would come along with dog ownership. They knew that, being kids, we would quickly grow bored of being the main caregivers of the dog and end up neglecting it. So, we were not allowed a dog right away. I think they knew that eventually they would end up caving in, but they tried to hold out for as long as possible.

One day, when we were in Montreal visiting my Opa and extended family, my dad came home with a boxer puppy. He was so small that he could fit in the palm of my hand. My mom was not thrilled with his decision, mostly because my dad hadn't told her that he was getting the dog. My dad had gone to the pet store to get a bird and came home with a puppy. It took her a little time to warm up to the change in plans.

My sisters and I had no problem falling in love with that puppy, and we played with him non-stop. My sister had a jacket with the character Wiley Coyote on it. I saw the jacket and suggested that we name him Wiley. Eventually, his name became Willie because we decided that was cuter.

Willie was a bundle of joy for us. He was such an amazing dog, so smart and loving, but there was also the rambunctiousness and excitability that would mean he often escaped to a nearby park. There were teacher and students at the Elmcrest Public School who would regularly call my mom to report Willie in the field.

As I got older, I decided to start training him and taking him for the daily long walks he required. Willie went through beginner obedience, novice, and advanced training. With a lot of hard work and practice, he passed with fly colors. Since he was so friendly and loving, the neighbors got to know him well.

My love for dogs continued to grow. When we went on vacation to Florida, my family would board Willie at a kennel called BRB K9 Obedience. Upon our return, my mom and I went to pick up Willie. Then my mom did something that took me totally by surprise, but I can honestly say was the start of my career with animals. She asked the owner if they were hiring. To my surprise, Sherri, the owner, said yes. I was given an opportunity to join their team. Several of the jobs I did involved animals. There were grooming salons, veterinary offices, and the humane society. I also learned to groom dogs and cats because it is my passion. Many people need to have their pets cared for, but they don't have the time to do it themselves. I enjoyed being in this world of caring for animals.

So, when the opportunity presented itself for me to own a pet grooming business, I took it. While I knew how to groom animals, there were many aspects of the early stages of business ownership that caught me by surprise.

Understanding the Potential Risk

Owning a business also comes with a level of risk. During the COVID-19 pandemic, for instance, businesses faced the challenge of customers being quarantined, supply chain disruptions, and shutdowns that made operating a business nearly impossible. You had to get creative and innovative, often pivoting to different opportunities, just so that your business could survive during the storm.

However, those storms can sometimes uncover opportunities that lead your business onto a path of considerable growth. It has been incredible watching restaurants find new ways to create revenue without having individuals sitting at tables and ordering food. Some have taken advantage of delivery where they did not have it in the past. Others have created meals that one just takes home and cooks, providing all the ingredients and instructions. The result is that their business was able to innovate for survival and, ultimately, success.

Why do I bring this up? Because owning a business means that you will have to weather all kinds of different storms. They might be external ones, like the pandemic or a natural disaster. Others might be internal, such as the changing of staff or growing to the point that you need to expand. Some business owners have found their industry changing so much that they needed to pivot in order to reach the next level. Innovation is also a wonderful way to pivot as an entrepreneur.

Business ownership means handling risk by learning how to pivot within these ever-changing circumstances. Part of learning to pivot means creating opportunities instead of waiting for them to come to you. Often, challenges become the necessity that fuels innovation, and that means circumstances can fuel your creativity. Take an everyday passion and turn it into a viable business venture. Think about areas where you could be considered an expert, and then start to build your business around that expertise.

Climbing a mountain also presents some risks; circumstances that cause you to pivot or get innovative. The point of the mountain climb is to reach the summit, whatever that might be. As a business owner, I dealt with various challenges during the early days, to the point where I am now ready for the transition into the next phase of my career.

For bonuses go to ...

Throughout these chapters, I will share with you some of my journey climbing mountains. Along the way, I will share how I took a pet grooming business and helped it thrive to the point that I have moved into the education realm, teaching others how to set up a successful pet grooming business. The student became the teacher, and I believe that you can also end up sharing your knowledge and experiences with others. That is part of building a legacy, but more about that later.

Mental Toughness to Keep Going

Another reason why owning a business is like climbing a mountain is that it also requires a certain mental toughness. In the early stages of my trip, I was focused on the sights and getting to know those in my group. Yet, as the climb began, I ended up relying more on my guides. They encouraged me to keep going, bolstering my will to conquer the mountain. There were times when I struggled to keep going, but the goal also kept my feet moving.

Even though, once I got to the top, all I wanted to do was come back down, the truth was that I had accomplished something incredible. It made me recognize that I could do more than I might have thought I was capable of accomplishing. There is a certain inner strength that you discover.

Owning a business can also uncover your inner strengths, and the toughness to keep going when the obstacles seem overwhelming. You will learn so much about yourself during the early days of setting up your business, but also as you help it to grow.

Years before I purchased my business and started my entrepreneurial career, I had a lot of insecurities. I was shy and rarely talked. My love of dogs and animals meant that I was more comfortable around them then I was around large crowds. While I acted like I didn't want my voice to be heard, the truth was the opposite. I did want my voice to be heard.

One day, I heard about a book called *The Secret*. I decided to pick it up and start reading. That was a critical decision in my life. Everything in that book ended up making a difference in my life. I realized that I could do just about anything if I put my mind to it. It ended up being such a huge part of my life that I would pick the book up when I was feeling down, allowing the contents to give me inspiration, or a boost.

The point is that your mental toughness can be developed, even if you have insecurities or concerns about taking the leap to owning a business. To climb over that obstacle, you need to seek out inspiration, be it in the form of books, podcasts, or speakers. Use opportunities to learn from experienced individuals in your field.

Even the school I have started, which helps to train individuals on how to open and operate a pet grooming salon, is based upon the idea that I have knowledge that I want to share with others, sharing my expertise within the industry.

For bonuses go to www.tanyaellis.com

Clearly, there are a variety of things that business owners encounter, especially during the early days and years. With that in mind, let's talk about one of my earliest lessons, which involved my wallet.

Chapter 2

Packing Your Backpack For Business

No mountain climber ever starts the journey without supplies. You cannot climb without food and shelter, but the most critical thing is water. I learned as I climbed that water was the most important thing. Part of my journey up the mountain included frequent stops for rest and water.

When you purchase a business, you also need supplies, particularly water. What is the water for any business? The reality is that no business can function without capital. You need it for purchasing supplies, hiring employees, marketing, renting a space for business, paying utilities, and so much more.

In the early days of your business, you likely sit down and create a budget based upon your business plan. There is a specific amount of capital, and it has to stretch to cover any number of early expenses. For my pet grooming business, there was the initial buildout of the space. It had to include a wet area and a dry one. There were tubs and mats to be put in, along with the sprayers that helped to wet the dogs and then rinse them once I finished their shampoo.

Then there was the dry area, filled with tables and supplies for cutting their hair, trimming nails, and combing them out. The drying area was where I took a wet dog and gave them the equivalent of a blowout. Plus, I needed to have storage for all the supplies, and a place for the dogs to hang out before and after their appointments. Then there was the retail center, waiting area, and front counter, where individuals could make appointments, pay for their dog's services, and also shop for things that they could use at home to keep their dogs looking great.

No matter how well you budget for your buildout, there are always going to be surprises. Plumbing that needs to be replaced or requires a cleanout. There might be delays regarding how soon various items will be available. Trying to schedule contractors and installers while you have a delay in getting tubs or tables can be challenging to say the least!

I quickly realized that there were going to be things that came up and, financially, I was not always going to be ready for them. Every business owner wishes they had more capital, especially during the startup phase. You are funding this business during a time when it is not able to bring in any funds. Even in the first weeks, as you have your first sales or appointments, you are still funding the business because it simply does not make enough to cover everything necessary for its operations.

Some business owners remember being open and not having one customer through the door. That means you had the costs of utilities, the space, employees, and no revenue to cover those expenses. Even when you create a contingency fund, it seems to drain much faster than you planned.

When you climb a mountain, your supplies seem heavy at first, because you are carrying a lot. As the climb continues, the backpack gets lighter because you start using up those supplies. Your finances for your business are similar in the beginning. It seems that you have a lot of capital available, but as you start using it, the bank account gets lighter and lighter.

Take Practice Steps to Manage Your Initial Investment

What can you do to manage your financial supplies, and those surprises? The first thing is to set a budget and stick to it. Hold yourself accountable for the money you spend. That means if you set aside a certain amount for flooring, then you need to stick to that amount.

When it comes to your buildout, be realistic regarding the types of materials you actually need. Invest in quality equipment that helps your business to function. After all, if you buy something of lesser quality just to save capital, you could end up finding yourself replacing it later, but also dealing with the loss of revenue that comes from downtime while equipment is being ordered and installed or repaired.

Also, look for durability. Designing your business, especially a pet grooming business, involves looking at materials in terms of how they will stand up to wear and tear. Some flooring options, for instance, are beautiful, but unlikely to stand up to regularly getting wet, or the scratches from dogs' nails. Being selective can end up benefiting your bottom line.

For bonuses go to ...

Additionally, you should have backups of critical equipment. For instance, if you plan on having several groomers working, then you will want to have at least two dryers and one backup dryer. Why? Because the reality is that life happens. Dryers need maintenance or repairs, and you still have clients coming in the front door. Not having backup equipment can mean that you lose revenue because you have to cancel appointments.

The water of your initial investment needs to be used strategically, but there are definitely places where you should prioritize your spending, as I illustrated above.

Setting the Goals for Your Business

Right from the beginning of my mountain climb, I had a goal of reaching the top. But as we climbed from day to day, my focus became reaching those smaller goals of reaching each camp and covering a certain distance.

In your business, you need the big lofty vision of what you want to ultimately achieve. Yet, before you can reach that vision, there will be smaller goals that you must complete. Early in my life, I found that writing down goals, dreams, and my vision of the future gave it more depth and clarity. I have always taken this very seriously, because I believe that when you write something down, it tends to come true. Writing down something as small as getting one new client per week can become a reality because, by putting it on paper, you bring that goal into focus.

I have had vision boards my whole life. It's funny because, when you go back and look at the goals you wrote down as part of your vision board, you will notice how many of those goals actually came true!

Usher says success is about dedication. You may not always be where you want to be, or doing what you want to do when you are on the journey, but you must be willing to have the vision and foresight necessary to reach that incredible ending.

Plus, making notes is a great way to implement what you have learned throughout your life. The brain registers it and incorporates it easier than when you just hear something. I think it is because writing involves more of your senses. Remember that every goal you set is putting you one step closer to reaching the top of your mountain!

Is Your Backpack Ready?

During my travels, I found that my journal was an important piece of equipment. I was able to record my feelings, experiences, and how everything was done. The truth is that my journal is now a place where someone else can learn about the adventure of mountain climbing. They would tap into my experience.

When it comes to filling your backpack, it is important to not just dive into creating a business without tapping into other resources. Many mistakes that you make during the early days of your business were made by someone else. They are not new, but you have the opportunity to avoid making them yourself.

For bonuses go to ...

To tap into those resources, consider looking for training opportunities. Allow those who have already been there to teach you what they learned. It gives you a chance to incorporate those lessons into how you run your business. Along the way, you will learn how to avoid expensive mistakes.

For instance, do you know how much tax you should be charging your customers? Should you be charging them tax at all? Knowing your state's tax laws for your type of business is key to avoiding potentially expensive fees and penalties.

When I created my school for pet grooming business owners, my goal was to teach them what to do and help them to avoid various mistakes that could end up costing them time and capital. The early days of my business meant working another job to help cover expenses while I built a clientele. It also gave me a chance to learn new skills, including those of management, customer service, and teamwork.

If you are ready to buy a pet grooming business or start one of your own, it is important to be prepared for unexpected expenses. After all, the early days of your business are going to be focused on marketing, and letting people know about your business and the services that you offer, as well as building up the right team to handle your clients as the business grows.

The problem is that the operations will still require funding during these stages. I encourage you to set a realistic budget for early operations and marketing. Included in those costs is the cost of designing the right logo for your business.

I remember coming up with my logo like it was yesterday. I was doodling on a piece of paper with a pencil, producing a few different ideas. My neighbor, Steve, had one of his employees who was in graphic design create my very first logo. It was pink, with five paw pads, and five different animals on it: a dog, guinea pig, cat, rabbit, and iguana.

With your logo in place, you can put your marketing hat on to create your first set of marketing tools, which typically includes flyers and business cards, although it can eventually expand to include commercials and social media ads. Let me be clear here that in the early stages of your business, word of mouth is key. I remember my parents, family, and friends spreading the word about my grooming business. But I was also actively talking to people about that business. There was one thing I did which was a little different, but it was effective. I would go into Starbucks and order under my business name. Then they would announce it to let me know my drink was ready.

I would also go to the local vet clinics and network with them. If there were connections I could make with the businesses in the area, I did it, thus creating a working relationship that ended up benefiting both our businesses. Basically, my early marketing strategy was to talk to everyone I knew. The goal was to make my business the first one that came to mind if they were trying to find a groomer.

For bonuses go to ...

Get Inspired by Others

One of the things that I noted as I began working in grooming is the importance of networking with others in the industry who are providing different services to your target customers. I had started working for the BRB K9 obedience, for Sherri Davis. Sherri was smart and inspiring, and the reason why I wanted to start my own business. I wanted to be like her, with people looking up to me like they did Sherri.

I learned so much about myself working there. Sherri had so much knowledge and I was like a sponge, wanting to learn everything and anything I could about dogs. We went to dog shows together, where I was introduced to a lot of new ideas. I ended up teaching puppy training, novice classes, and grooming, and I answered phones, provided excellent customer service, cleaned up, and fed dogs. It was a place where I got to do every job in the business at one point or another. That was the opportunity of a lifetime for me.

During high school, I was able to work for the Southdown Animal Clinic for my co-op placement. Doctor Warren was the owner, but I worked with another veterinarian named Dr. Roberta Vietch. She was like a mentor to me. I learned so much about how to care for animals. The cleanliness throughout the clinic taught me how important it was to make sure that I had a high level of cleanliness in my grooming salon.

Having these individuals in my life gave me a great start to understanding how to work in my business, and what roles I needed to fill.

Pick a Passion

Getting ready for any climb requires understanding where you want to go, but also having the drive to get there, no matter what the obstacles. For me, understanding where I want to go is wrapped up in finding my passion. I encourage others who want to open a business not to pick it based only on the financial benefits. It is also important to make sure that it aligns with your passion.

I say this because, when I speak with people, they are confused about what type of business to start. They know that they want the freedom that comes with being a business owner. Your passion can also make it easy to choose what you want to do.

For me, it was easy to choose to work with dogs. It was what I was born to do. There was really nothing else that made sense to me. Before you decide to go into business for yourself, spend some time figuring out what makes you happy, and what you always go back to. Can you see yourself doing it for a living?

Passion is what drives every human on the planet. "Follow your passion, be prepared to work hard and sacrifice, and above all, don't let anyone limit your dreams," said Donovan Bailey. Finding your passion can also help you to stay the course when it gets challenging. If you have a passion for working with animals, then the industry is wide open for you to find a business that allows you to spend time with them.

Once you know what your passion is, you have to act on it. Don't allow fear of potential failure to stop you from pursuing your passion. You should always follow your heart, because your heart always knows the way. If you think about it too much, then your head will get in the way.

Instead of focusing on what potential obstacles you might encounter, focus on how you can integrate your passion into your business. I felt blessed to know what my passion was at an early age. My parents also supported my passion without judgment.

Never assume that your passion cannot be part of your financial future. Instead, allow your creativity and inventiveness to help you find a path forward.

As you can see, there are a variety of things that you need before you start a new business. But like the backpack that I put together before I started to climb the mountain, if you take the time to prepare, then you can truly start off your business on the right foot. Now let's dive into how you can put your business on a solid foundation during the early stages, to give it the best chance to grow.

Chapter 3

Building a Solid Foundation

Owning a business involves a significant amount of time and effort. You are constantly juggling many different balls. After all, you have to get the customers in the door, give them a positive experience so they want to come back, handle the administrative tasks, schedule employees, order supplies, pay bills, strategic planning, and more. The list could go on forever.

While juggling all those balls in the early days of your business, you want to look to the future. There will be a time when the company has grown to the point that you cannot be everywhere. Before becoming stressed out and overwhelmed, it is essential to have a plan in place to build your personnel to the point that you have a solid foundation for the future of your business.

Finding the Right Guide

During the initial stages of my climb, there was so much to see and do, but as I climbed higher, I had to rely increasingly on my guides. Not only were the guides a source of encouragement, but they also gave me the benefit of their practical wisdom. These men had done this climb many times, so they were the experts.

For bonuses go to ...

Finding experts in your field is a critical way to get your business off to the right start before you even open your doors. You are tapping into the knowledge that they have, from the mistakes that they have already made. There is no reason that you shouldn't take advantage of their wisdom and avoid those pitfalls yourself.

When I read *The Secret*, I was gaining wisdom about how to turn my dreams into my reality. But I also noticed that there were business books that focus on the nuts and bolts of operating a business, marketing a business, and creating a business plan. Basically, head into any bookstore's business section and start your research.

While I won't go into each of those topics here, it is essential that you tap into the resources available, because that can help you to identify areas where you might be weak, and where you need to work on your skills or find others with those skill sets and create a professional relationship.

Why is that so important? When you are growing a business, it is a common misconception that you need to do everything yourself. You might be looking to save money, or just want to make sure that everything is done correctly. The problem is that, eventually, you end up not having time for the important parts of your business, including strategic growth.

Even if you have done the research and tapped into the wisdom of others, you still might be hindering yourself because of a mindset that is based on a fear of letting go and trusting others to care for your business.

It is your baby, something that is growing from a dream into a viable reality. To conquer that fear, let's talk about what it means to change your mentality, and practical ways to do just that.

Changing Your Mentality

The mentality that you cannot delegate or need to do everything yourself to save money could cost your business. One of the things that you quickly realize when you own a business is how challenging it is to be everywhere at once.

Repeatedly, you find out that there are not enough hours in the day to care for your customers, stock shelves, place orders for supplies, clean, do your accounting, manage the schedule, pay bills, check out the reviews online and reply, look after marketing, design marketing materials, and the list goes on and on.

I remember the early days of running my business in my parents' basement. My marketing strategy was heavily focused on word-of-mouth advertising. I was also working another job, then scheduling my pet grooming clients around that schedule. It was a lot of work! Plus, I still had all the demands of my personal life, family, and friends. To say I was stretched thin is an understatement.

Eventually, I realized that I needed to start thinking about my time differently. We all have to come to this realization if we expect our businesses to be successful. First, recognize that time you spend caring for customers limits your time to work on marketing and growing your client base.

Let's stop for a minute and put a number to your time. Give it value based on how much you can earn in an hour. Then use that to help you determine the priority of your tasks for the day. If you have ten clients scheduled for one day, but only three for the next two days, then marketing needs to move up the list, but you still need to care for those scheduled clients. Delegating tasks that others can easily do gives you the ability to focus on the tasks that are uniquely suited to you as the owner.

Taking the step of delegating tasks might not be easy at first. After all, you have been juggling everything for a long time. But for your business to grow and get past that first basecamp, you need to delegate.

Early delegation involves hiring employees, training them, and trusting them with specific tasks. You might also find that this delegation mentality bleeds into your personal life. I know individuals who hate to clean, and taking time to do it keeps them away from what they enjoy. So, they delegate that task to someone else, freeing up their time to use it more effectively.

I mention this because we all have a task list that we put off as long as possible. Eventually, we begrudgingly take care of the list, but we are thinking about the other stuff we want to be doing.

I want you to shift your mentality and start finding ways to get that task list done without you actually spending the time. By refocusing your mindset, it becomes easier to delegate and even opt out of doing tasks altogether. Do not focus on having to be busy every second of the day, thinking that is the only measure of your productivity.

The truth is that your productivity is measured by how your activities contribute to your growth or the growth of your business. When I was climbing that mountain, I didn't focus on keeping busy every second. I took opportunities to rest and recharge, and then I was ready for the next stage of the climb. I didn't assume that because I was resting, I was not making progress.

The reality is that mental toughness is necessary when you open a business, but don't let your mental toughness force you to exhaust yourself and question whether your business is worth the effort.

Instead, get your business off the ground and start looking for ways to delegate responsibility so that you can have time to recharge. It is key to making your way to the summit and also to help your business grow. This is the mentality that will help your business to thrive in the future, because fear of losing control will no longer be handicapping you.

What You Don't Know Can Slow You Down

When I started out in the pet grooming world, I had a small tribe of individuals who spoke about my services and gave people my number. It was a fantastic way for me to grow my small business. On the other hand, I also knew my target customers and could reach them through other like-minded people.

The mistake many people make when starting a new business is not knowing their target audience. It means their marketing efforts are less than stellar, and they often end up not reaching those customers that would truly benefit from the services and products they are offering.

How can you determine what your target market is and how to reach them? First, start by asking yourself what you want to offer. I focused on offering pet grooming but, later, I would end up adding a small retail section, making it easier for my customers to get treats or a new collar and leash. It added a level of value because it was convenient. How can you add value for your potential clients? Is your business idea based upon making their lives easier? What problem are you solving for the customer that makes them want to order from your business? If you can't find evidence of demand for your idea, then it might not be the right business for you.

Determining the answers to these questions can help you to figure out the best way to connect with those individuals and help them to find your business, thus giving you a greater opportunity to complete the sale.

Therefore, even though you are eager to get the doors of your business open, spend time defining your target customer. Keep it clear in your mind as you develop your marketing materials. Start-up businesses can rush into marketing ideas without pondering how it connects them with their target market.

You might be thinking to yourself, "How do I define my target market and determine if someone is interested in purchasing what I have to offer?"

One way is to conduct market research. You have defined your idea but now you need to learn if that idea is even viable. Conducting surveys, holding focus groups, and researching SEO and public data are just a few ways that you can do market research to find out whether there is demand for your business.

For pet grooming, it is important to find data that gives you an idea of how many pet owners there are in your area and how many grooming salons are already in business in that area. That will help you determine if there is demand for your business, or if the area is already saturated.

Market research is part of what defines your target customer's needs, preferences, and behaviors. Using a competitive analysis, you can better understand the opportunities and limits of your market. Plus, as you grow your knowledge of their behaviors, you can focus your marketing efforts more effectively.

Think about it this way. If you know that you are targeting pet owners who regularly get their dogs groomed, then you want to go where they regularly get information. It might involve getting onto the neighborhood social media boards or spending time at the local dog parks. You wouldn't waste time advertising in restaurants that aren't pet-friendly or apartment complexes that do not allow pets.

Doing this market research can also help you to find the gaps in the market, giving you some ways to add value for your customers and also make you stand out from the other grooming salons in the area. Perhaps you can offer doggie daycare, giving people a place to bring their dog for exercise and socialization. You might also be able to host an obedience class, depending on the space you have. The point is that market research can help you focus your business and find your target audience, as well as give you a strong path forward to find your niche.

Another mistake that I see people making is doing market research early in the life of their business and then essentially opting out of it as the business starts to take off. Why is this a mistake? Because your target customers can be shifting, presenting new opportunities for you to solve their problems. The demand for what you offer could also be changing, meaning that you need to pivot your business.

For instance, when an area struggles economically, individuals are most likely to start cutting what they deem to be luxuries. That means pushing back hair appointments, limiting vacations or activities with a higher price tag, and even cutting back on how frequently they have their pets groomed. With that in mind, how can you offer value to your customers, thus keeping your business afloat?

Businesses might opt to offer extra services or create an à la carte menu, helping individuals to get the services they need at a price that fits their budget. Instead of them not bringing in their pets at all, you could give them a limited grooming option that still allows your business to maintain a stream of revenue.

It is that level of creativity that is key to both a start-up and a company that has been in business for years. Do not think that once your business has clients, you no longer need to keep marketing, innovating, or pivoting. If you stop doing these things, your business can suffer.

A business that is not growing is not thriving, it is slowly dying. I focus on this because so many owners get trapped into the daily grind of their business that they stop doing the things that made it grow in the first place. Your customers are changing, and their needs are changing too. Are you keeping up or ignoring the changes that are happening because you are comfortable with the old way of operating?

I want to interject here that technology is impacting every industry, even pet grooming. The traditional way of scheduling an appointment by making a telephone call is giving way to apps that allow you to see what is offered, book an appointment, and even pay through the app.

Your customers are looking for convenience. Don't let your business fall behind because you opt to ignore the technology that could make you more appealing to your target customer. As you can see, there is a lot that can be involved just in the early stages of opening a business, and its early growth.

My school for those looking to open a pet grooming business is about more than just helping them understand the various aspects involved in its operations, but also helping them to see the bigger picture. You need skills and tools to grow the business, but you also need to have a guide, someone who can give directions when you are struggling or not sure how to get past the plateau.

Even after years of working and growing my business, I still saw areas where I needed to grow. With that in mind, let's talk about how to get to the next basecamp with your business and how to incorporate your long-term goals.

Chapter 4

Setting Goals to Reach the Summit

Part of the challenge of climbing a mountain is the work that you need to put in as you get closer to the top. It doesn't get easier; if anything, the climb only gets harder. Basecamps are critical, because they give you a chance to rest up, power up with quality nutrition, and share experiences with others to get encouragement to keep going. I remember spending time journaling, as a way to keep myself motivated and also to help my mind settle so I could sleep.

When you start a new business, there is a rush of excitement, which can often propel you past those first bumps in the journey. However, as your business begins to grow, you are now faced with greater challenges that require more from you and your team. How can you create basecamps that will help you to reach your larger goal, which is at the top of the summit?

Setting Goals for Success

Building and growing a business is all about goal setting. In the early days, those goals were small and likely included reaching a certain number of customers per day, having sales at specific amounts so that you had enough to cover the operations costs and payroll, as well as finding an affordable way to get people

For bonuses go to ...

talking. (Hint: Order Starbucks and put the name of your business on your order!)

However, as those smaller goals are achieved and your business becomes more stable, you may need to establish larger goals that are reflective about what you want to achieve with this business, both personally and professionally.

I know many business owners initially start their companies with the goal of being financially independent and having more time to spend with family, loved ones, or on causes that speak to their hearts and minds.

However, once they get involved in the day-to-day running of their business, the initial goals that motivated them to start the business begin to fade. Then it becomes more challenging to stay motivated to continue running the business.

This is where having a clear picture of what you want to achieve and outlining the goals to get there becomes so critical. It is your map, the way you stay focused on the summit. That outline of goals can be a great way to set the priorities of your business on a weekly, monthly, and annual basis.

How do these goals relate to basecamps?

As you set your goals and begin to achieve them, you can use regular check-ins (basecamps) to make sure you are still on target to achieve your long-term goal or summit.

How can you do this?

Start by having a regular team meeting, discussing what the priorities are for the week, as well as how they relate to the overall goals for the month. Help your team to see where they are on track and where there might be a need for changes, either in procedures or policies. Perhaps you can also use these meetings to identify where additional training might be necessary.

Notice that these meetings end up being a way to keep your team focused, as well as playing a part in recharging you and your team for the next stage of your journey.

Another aspect of this type of basecamp is that you can use them to measure your progress to date and how much further you have to go. When I reached a basecamp, I knew I was higher up the mountain and that much closer to achieving my goal of reaching the summit.

Why is it important to measure your results and make adjustments where necessary? Simply put, you will not be motivated enough to reach the summit if you do not take the time to understand what you have already achieved, and what it will take for you to reach the next milestone in your journey.

How do you measure the journey? There are so many different ways, depending on your business. However, don't just check a few boxes, input some information, and then never look at it again. Use those reports to assist you in analyzing where your business is right now, and how you can improve.

For bonuses go to ...

Perhaps you are meeting all your goals for connecting with new customers, but you are not retaining them. As a pet business, repeat customers are critical to the long-term viability of your business. By setting some key measurements into your business, then you can find the areas where improvement might be necessary, make the changes, and reap the benefits.

However, there are ways to measure literally every aspect of your business and it can get to the point that you are overwhelming yourself with data. To avoid that, consider creating a business plan. Once you do, it will give you the key areas to focus on, measuring how they align with your goals. How do you create a business plan and why is it necessary?

As I share the answer to this question, recognize that your dream is not to keep your business running from week to week and wearing yourself out in the process. So, let's dive into the business plan and how you can use it to better define the journey of your business.

Define the Journey With a Business Plan

How can you be sure that you are setting the right goals to achieve what you want? First, sit down with your business plan, which will serve as a guide for how you will manage your company. It can also serve as a way to keep the leadership of your business on the same page.

If you don't have one, now is a great time to outline one. Set out what you want the business to become. Is it supposed to be a company that generates $10 million dollar a year in revenue, or one that simply generates $1 million dollars a year? Your business might be on a smaller scale, and your goal might simply be to achieve $500,000 a year. Whatever the goal, your business plan needs to be part of defining the steps to achieve it. What will it take to get there? That can help you to define yearly sales goals, since each year will help you build to your long-term revenue goals.

Once you have the larger sales goals, then you can break down what is necessary to achieve them, including funding that you might need. Think about the personnel you need, the number of customers, and even the daily revenue. With each of those areas, there are still even more steps that must be taken.

Your plan should also include strategies to respond to changes in your market or to help you track current projects. This is also the place to establish goals and metrics that will end up defining whether you are successful or not. Understand that as your business grows or there are significant changes in how you operate, updating your business plan will be necessary. Think of it as refining your vision as you get closer to your summit.

There are a few critical parts that can be found in a business plan, no matter how formal or informal it might be.

First, there is the executive summary, which introduces the plan to your audience, whether it is your team, a financial institution, or a potential investor. Make sure that it is clear, but also reflects the voice and culture of your company.

Secondly, you need a company overview, which gives the history of your company. Keep this bio short and to the point. It can include history, significant accomplishments, and legal data. If you have a mission statement, then add it here. Remember, this is where you are conveying your company's story, so make sure you do it effectively.

The third part is your product or service information. Detail what your company actually does, including how your solution benefits your customers, how you produce that solution, and whether it is proprietary or not. If you are running a pet business, likely there is not going to be much in the way of proprietary information. But it is important that you think of your business as a unique offering in the market, instead of just one of the crowd. Writing about your products and services can be one way to do just that.

The fourth part involves your marketing or sales plan. While you don't need to get into all the finer details, but you should outline who your target demographic is and how you plan to reach them.

The last two pieces are your financials and organizational structure, which defines who the key players are within your business. Now you might have additional pieces, depending on your intended audience.

As I work with individuals who are creating businesses, I see them so focused on just paying their operating expenses or getting a salary that they never spend any time thinking about how to grow the business. Too often, these owners live in survival mode, and that is a horrible place to be. Your business always seems to be limping along. Over time, you get so frustrated that you decide to give up, sell the business, and move on to something else.

I don't want you to lose sight of your dream because your business never gets past the financial stage of being new. Instead, I want you to create a business plan and use it to choose goals that will help you achieve what you set out in that plan.

Remember the Importance of a Network

Another amazing aspect of basecamp was how it helped me to connect with others on the same journey. We could encourage each other and talk about our experiences in a meaningful way.

For new business owners, tapping into a network can provide you a greater level of encouragement, give you practical ideas for addressing challenges, and more. Not only that, when you are part of a network, you position yourself to help others.

Over the years, I have met with other business owners, particularly those in the pet industry. I recognized that we face a lot of similar obstacles, but each of us is trying to solve it on our own, unable to tap into a collective wisdom. That is why I find networking to be so vital. It is not about competition; it is about helping to lift each other up and create a thriving industry.

How do you network? Start by looking in your local area for business events. Your Chamber of Commerce is a great place to start. There you can meet up with other business owners and build connections. However, it is not just about what you get out of it, but what you can offer others. Did you have a particular problem and come up with an innovative solution? Be open to sharing that solution. By coming together, local businesses can begin to thrive, and the community as a whole can benefit.

Another way to network is by educating yourself. I worked in the pet industry for many years, and I saw that individuals who wanted to start pet grooming businesses did not have the tools to be successful. There is a significant investment of time and money when you start out, so the pressure to be successful is on.

However, you can end up wasting valuable resources simply because you do not know what you do not know. With that in mind, I have started the work of providing an education for individuals who want to run these businesses. I believe that part of networking is also about giving back. When I teach others how to be successful, then I am not taking away from my business, but empowering others to grow their own.

The beauty of caring for animals is that individuals are always going to have pets that need care. The market is large, which makes it a wonderful business opportunity, with plenty of opportunities to specialize. Some groomers prefer to focus on older animals, while others provide exercise and play options for their clients.

Building a network and getting involved in your local business community can allow you to see where the needs are and what niche you can fill. Seeking educational opportunities can also be a way to meet other like-minded business individuals, while also growing your bank of knowledge.

As you can see, basecamps are about education, connection, and recharging. They help you to see where you are, how far you have come and where you are going. Now, I want to zero in on how to grow your business during challenging times.

Chapter 5

Have You Hit the Wall?

When we were more than halfway up the mountain, I was definitely feeling fatigued, both physically and mentally. I wasn't getting much sleep at all. Each camp was vital for me to recharge, even though I was having a harder time sleeping as we got closer to the top.

The challenges we faced as we got closer to the summit were harder on me, because I was feeling the effects of the climb. Machu Picchu, for example, was really steep in some areas. I am afraid of heights. Can you imagine that?

Perhaps you have been in business for a while, and everything has been going well. You have been achieving your goals and starting to see progress. Then, just like that, your business is hit with a curveball, something that threatens everything that you have worked so hard to build.

One of the biggest curveballs to hit businesses in the last two years has been the COVID-19 pandemic. Initially, businesses were faced with either closing their doors or finding creative ways to provide their services. Businesses were forced to pivot in a variety of ways.

For bonuses go to ...

Restaurants, for instance, were unable to serve their customers traditionally, so some chose to increase delivery options or even to offer meal kits that could be purchased and prepared at home.

It was not easy, by any stretch of the imagination. Supply chains were disrupted, and finding workers became more challenging. Businesses find that they are not responding to one challenge, but multiple challenges. It is like being in a boxing ring with a professional boxer and being new to the sport. You feel like you are getting kicked around a lot!

After a certain point, you just start feeling overwhelmed. If challenges are coming at you over and over again, you might wonder if you can be successful. I don't want you to give up!

With that in mind, I want to share a few skills that I believe business owners must have to survive and thrive during the hardest parts of the climb with their business.

Imagination

When you decided to open your business, you likely had a very clear vision of what you wanted to achieve. It was a movie playing in your head. What fueled that vision was your imagination.

However, as time goes on and the daily grind starts to wear you down, your vision can grow dim. Problems can become obstacles with no solutions, simply because your brain narrows its focus, and your imagination gets drowned out.

To get your imagination ramped up again, spend a few minutes each day bringing that original vision into focus. Be specific in the details and make it so realistic in your head that you feel as if you are already there. This regular routine helps to activate your imagination. When your imagination is working for you, it is easier to think outside of the box and find the right solutions for your business.

It can be a struggle not to feel stuck from time to time, especially when the challenges facing your business are not of your own making. Think about the challenges created by the COVID-19 pandemic. Businesses were shut down or working with minimal staff and supplies. Even once the worst of the lockdowns was over, supply chain disruptions continued to plague businesses around the world.

With that struggle, imagination is key, because you use it to envision the best course for your business in light of those challenges that you cannot control. Doing so will keep you from feeling helpless, but also enable you to make changes or adjustments in what you can control. For example, a friend of mine who owns a paint studio in Port Credit, called the Studio Paint Bar, pivoted. She added a patio and appetizers, drinks and sometimes live music; she changed her business and made it a really fun and upbeat new adventure. Julia Chatterji is awesome, and I really admire her tenacity.

Be Able to Pivot

Along with your imagination, you need to be open to change and willing to pivot your business when the situation calls for that. Pivoting means being able to adapt the model of your business to meet the current realities of your market.

In the pandemic, for instance, restaurants found themselves with inventory and no customers. What did many of them do? They pivoted their business model, providing takeout and delivery options that were not available in the past. Others opted to create meals that people could purchase and then take home and cook themselves, thus becoming a defacto grocery store.

The point is that they developed another way to serve their customers and also bring in revenue. Some businesses that pivoted in this way found a new niche that created growth opportunities. Without a willingness or ability to pivot, none of that would be possible.

Don't be afraid of change. See it as a natural extension of your customer service. After all, our goal is that our customers have a great experience and bring their dogs back. Your customer service says a lot about the type of business you run and the values that shape your decisions. People will associate your business with being "good" or "bad" depending on their experience with you or your staff. Ensuring your employees deliver the best possible experience at every customer interaction will help your business to build loyalty.

Part of being able to pivot means knowing what your customers need and want. What are the problems that they might be having? Can you offer a solution? You can ask your customers through surveys or response cards.

The point is that by knowing what your customers want, you can put yourself in the position to take advantage of the opportunities for growth. Plus, when challenging situations arise, you will have the ability to pivot, because you know what your customers need and are willing to pay for.

Delegate for Growth

As an owner, it can be a source of anxiety the first time you delegate, but it is crucial that you do so. Your business can only grow so far with the current staff and infrastructure that you have created. Eventually, hiring and building up your ability to take on more appointments is one path to growth. Leading your team means focusing on the big picture and the long-term growth of the business.

If you are delegating the duties that do not need your direct involvement, you are buying back time for other tasks that contribute to the growth. To avoid taking on tasks that you could delegate, make an appointment with yourself once a month, so you can audit how you are spending your time. If you are spending a lot of time backing up your team with menial tasks, then you are not creating new opportunities for growth.

Delegating is like a muscle. The more you do it, the easier it will get. Now that being said, you should have some processes in place for accountability. That will make sure that individuals are doing their jobs and not taking advantage as you move into a leadership role, instead of being involved in every day-to-day interaction with the customers.

Innovate to Build the Next Stage

One of the reasons that I believe in innovation is because the initial offerings of your business will only take it so far. Then you will hit the proverbial wall. The earnings will plateau, while expenses continue to increase.

By knowing what interests your target customers, you can start to innovate ways that your business could address those interests. Envision the next summit for your business and then start taking steps to reach it. One thing that is true about business ownership is that you can envision a summit, but once you reach it, another one is always beckoning. Climbing a mountain takes mental and physical endurance, but it also takes the ability to see the goal and the willpower to attain it.

In your business, you have a vision of what you want to create and how you want to impact your community. Over time, innovation allows you to reshape that vision and set new goals. Those who innovate are the ones who can find ways to adjust during the storms and keep their business afloat.

As I climbed the mountain, there were shifts in the weather that meant adjusting how fast I climbed or how frequently I rested. It was still possible to reach the top, but adjustments had to be made.

Innovation is a critical tool in making any shifts or adjustments because when you innovate, you start thinking outside of the box, not looking at how everyone else is doing it. When I work with other pet groomers, I am always learning new things. Why? Because they come up with new and different ways to accomplish tasks and also keep their customers happy. I don't see them as competitors, but another opportunity to learn.

If you have innovative members of your team, encourage them to share their ideas. Weekly team meetings can be a great way to discuss challenges, brainstorm solutions, and tap into the innovative ideas of those on your team. Leadership is important but even more vital is being a thought leader, one with a heart to innovate.

Create Consistent Lines of Communication

Your staff is likely to be small at first, so communication can be easier to accomplish. However, as your business and team grows, maintaining the lines of communication gets more complicated. With that in mind, let's talk about some practical ways you can maintain communication lines and keep operations consistent, whether you are there or not.

First, make weekly staff meetings part of your routine. It can be a great way for you to address the whole team regarding any policy or procedural changes, and you can also answer any questions that the team may have. If there are issues they noticed, this can be a great way for them to share those. An example would

For bonuses go to ...

be the laundry is not consistently getting done because everyone is busier and that means they are running short of towels. By knowing about these things, you can get a process in place to address it.

Not only will the team know that you care about what is going on in the daily operations, but they will also feel more committed to the team because their ideas and concerns are being heard.

Secondly, create procedures for the team to bring specific concerns or problems to your attention. After all, an issue might be sensitive, and it would not be something you want to deal with in a team meeting. Perhaps setting up office hours for your staff or doing a bi-weekly check-in with the individuals on your team can give them a place to discuss concerns but also for you to give them feedback, both positive and constructive.

Finally, make sure there is a book of the updated policies and procedures, which should be easily available for everyone to reference. Doing so will mean that you can keep the team on the same page, instead of creating confusion.

Climbing the mountain involves regular communication with your guide and fellow climbers. Without their regular conversations and encouragement, I am not sure I would have made it to the top of Killi or the end of the Inca trail on Machu Picchu. In your business, that same communication is also key to making sure that your team is successful.

www.tanyaellis.com

Being Proactive to Keep Your Team Running Smoothly

Your business is likely full of protocols and procedures meant to address any eventuality. The purpose is to have seamless daily operations. Yet, no matter what you try to anticipate, there will always be something that comes up, creating a roadblock for your team.

As a result, you can end up being reactive because you are dealing with an angry customer, so you put measures in place to make sure the problem never happens again. However, those changes might only reflect a fraction of the challenges your team is facing and they might end up making things worse.

Therefore, you need to build some flexibility into your fixes, focusing instead on the context and then providing your team with what is necessary to success. That means recognizing that not every fix solves every problem. Thus, you end up being proactive and giving your team the weapons necessary to handle issues without needing you to interfere or serve as the referee.

All of these aspects and skills are part of the large role of leader. You serve as the focal point of your company. No matter what happens, your reaction shapes the culture and brings the purpose of the business to life. Your leadership style is what reminds the team of its purpose. Don't just assume that a sign on the wall is enough. Your strength as a leader can be measured by how many people are behind you and believe in the purpose as you defined it.

For bonuses go to www.tanyaellis.com

You are a source of inspiration, but you won't be much of one if you cannot interact well with others. Emotional intelligence is being able to perceive the emotions of others, but also manage your own emotional reactions. Being comfortable with yourself and aware of your values will make it easier to decide what to do, even under stress.

Never underestimate the importance of emotional intelligence as you lead your team. It could be the difference between success and constantly looking to hire because you are rotating team members in and out.

When you develop all these different skills as a business owner and leader, you give yourself the ability to overcome the challenges that your business might face. Instead of hitting the wall, you are going to be able to pivot or innovate to keep your business on track.

Now, let's talk about setting goals for your business in the years ahead.

Chapter 6

Growth is Never-Ending

Even after reaching the top of the mountain on my first climb, I realized that there was still more that I could and more I wanted to accomplish. I ended up traveling and climbing another mountain. The ability to view the world from the top of a mountain is an experience that I will never forget.

The same can be said of your business. In the early days, you were likely struggling in many different areas as you learned the ropes. Perhaps you reached out to your network or just learned through trial and error. After a while, you reached a level of success. It might be regular sales and a modest profit at the end of the year. However, now that you have achieved that success, you might be wondering if this is all that there is.

The reality is that for a business to be truly successful, there needs to be a focus on sustainable growth. There are practical ways that you can measure your growth through sales and revenue, but when it comes to growing your business, more is required.

For bonuses go to ...

Your Dreams Are the Goals

When you started this business, it was because you had a specific financial or personal goal that you wanted to achieve by being your own boss. Perhaps that initial goal has been achieved. Now it is time for you to set a new goal, one that focuses on where you want to go next.

Business goals are the things you anticipate accomplishing in a defined period of time. Those goals can be for the company as a whole, or for specific areas or departments. Whatever these goals are, they likely represent the larger purpose of your business. They can even have broad outcomes, allowing them to be less specific, at least initially.

As the leader of your team, your goals set the tone and purpose for the entire business. When you don't have a goal, the business itself begins to flounder. Once you achieve one dream, it is time to think of a new one and begin mapping out the steps to achieve that dream.

Setting business goals provides a way for you to measure success, keep your employees on the same page with a clear understanding of how you are making decisions to reach those goals, and ensure that your business stays on track.

This is why taking time to look at the bigger picture is so critical. After all, you can end up focusing solely on the day-to-day operations and wake up years from now in the same place, having only achieved a limited level of success.

When you take a step back from the daily operations, you can start to see where you want to business to go and what you hope to achieve in the next year, the next five years, and even the next ten years. This is where you map out the course of your business, creating action steps that your team can follow.

Perhaps your dream is building a business that can be franchised, thus allowing you to grow your business through multiple locations. In that case, you need to build protocols and processes that you have tested so customers get a similar experience regardless of what location they go to. Think about your favorite fast-food joint. Likely, it is part of a franchise. Yet, whether you go to one in your hometown or across the country, the experience is similar, and the food tastes the same. Why? Because they built procedures, protocols, and processes that could be easily replicated.

The same would be true if that is what you want for the next iteration of your business. There are other options, including reaching a specific annual revenue that would indicate it is time to sell your business.

The point is that without these goals, you will increase sales, but your business will lack direction. The question is how to create that foresight. Let's dive into some of the ways that you can develop it.

Be Aware of Blind Spots

There is so much technology in the world today, and with all the knowledge at our fingertips, it can be easy to think that you can come up with solutions to problems as they appear. The truth is that, as a business owner, you can never foresee every challenge or issue, and there isn't always going to be a YouTube® tutorial.

The problems you can't foresee end up popping up in what I like to call your blind spots. Those are the places where you can't envision the problem, let alone a solution. How can you limit the blind spots? Start by recognizing that, since you can't foresee everything, tapping into your team is critical. They can be a great resource of problems and solutions, thus helping you to see what you didn't notice before.

Let's talk about the franchise idea again. You might have put all the protocols together, but your team might be able to run through them and point out gaps that you haven't thought of. This will also assist you in addressing potential blind spots before they become an issue. The result will be a better franchise product.

Essentially, as a business owner, never assume that you know everything or that you can prepare for every contingency. Ultimately, there will be blind spots, but by using the various tools available, including the insight of your team, your mentor, and your network, you can reduce those blind spots.

Do You Have Goals or Objectives?

Another way to develop your business forecasting is by utilizing goals and objectives. Business objectives are those clearly defined and measurable steps that you and your team take to reach your broader goals. Objectives are naturally very specific, easily tracked, and easy to define.

Business goals define what your purpose is, and the objectives define the how. Your goals are a broad directional arrow, with the objectives providing the directions using clearly actionable steps.

As you achieve objectives, you are collecting data about how you did as a company. That information is key to outlining your future objectives, but also to determine if these objectives are taking you closer to your goal or not.

To determine the best objectives, you need to create goals for your business. Perhaps you had goals at the beginning, but over time, you lost track of what you were trying to accomplish. Here is a chance to get back on the path toward defining the future of your business and determining how you want it to grow.

Setting goals starts by giving yourself a timeframe. What do you want to accomplish in the next six months, year, five years, and ten years? Obviously, the goals for the shorter timeframes should assist in moving you closer to the goals that you want to achieve over five or ten years. It is about creating a list of long-term and short-term goals, since both are key to the success of your business.

Once the goals are set down, then you can take your short-term goals and break them into actionable objectives. Those are the steps your team will take to reach the goal. When you are climbing a mountain, each basecamp is another goal achieved toward your long-term goal (reaching the summit). However, there are objectives that you achieve on your way to the next basecamp. These are measurable, such as making it to that tree you see in the distance. When you reach the tree, you can look back and see how much you have already accomplished. I remember a moment while climbing Machu Picchu when we were in a beautiful part of the climb and I looked over the edge and got a picture standing close to it; the trees, the dew and the scenery were stunning, and learning to get over my fear of heights was astounding.

In business, the actionable objectives are also a great way to see how far you have come, as well as helping you to determine whether you are getting closer to your goal or if your objectives need to be shifted.

The challenge can often be that in order to keep yourself on target to achieve your goals, your objectives need to be measurable. For instance, one of your goals might be to increase your presence on social media. You wouldn't state your objective to be "post on social media regularly." After all, regularly is not defined by a specific schedule and there is no way to measure this objective.

Instead, you would look to put specific numbers and a timeframe into place. You might determine that you want to post on social media three times a week for the next six weeks. That gives you a timeframe and something to measure. Later, when the six weeks is up, you can look at the accumulated data to analyze whether it was helpful to your marketing or not, and then make the necessary adjustments.

Recognize that these objectives will involve your team because they will be the ones that help you to complete the objectives. Check in with them about their progress on the objectives, and what challenges they might be facing. It can help you to make adjustments to the objectives, so you reach your short-term and long-term business goals.

Establishing timeframes gives you a way to measure your short-term goals to ensure that you are on track to meet them. Your objectives are the best way to do just that.

Since pet grooming involves being hands-on with customers and their precious pets, make sure that your goals and objectives reflect the customer experience you want them to have. Make sure that as you reach your goals, the customer experience is not suffering. When you start increasing the number of clients, there can be a level of pressure to get the animals in and out as quickly as possible, but doing so could end up negatively impacting the quality of your team's work.

Craft objectives that allow your team a realistic amount of time for each customer's pet but stay open to ways that you can improve overall. Here is one goal that you might have related to increasing the number of repeat customers that can be translated into actionable objectives.

First, the goal is to increase the number of repeat customers within three months.

For bonuses go to ...

Your actionable and measurable objectives could be the following:

- Increase the number of customers on the newsletter list by 5 each week.
- Set up a social media group for new and existing customers and post in the group 3 times a week.
- Reach out to past customers 3 times a week with current offers or a coupon.

Notice that each objective as a specific number of times that it must be done, and a clear way to implement them into the routine of your team. For instance, someone who is checking out can be asked if they would like to join the newsletter. Seeing who frequently comments on your social media group can help you to target posts to get them interested in making an appointment.

When it comes to growing a business, you need clear and actionable goals and objectives. Make sure you have a way to measure your progress. Once a goal is achieved, be sure to set a new one. Do not assume that once your goals are achieved, there is no place else for the business to go. You might be surprised to find that getting excited about your business and getting off the plateau begins with setting fresh goals.

Align Your Goals to Your Vision for Growth

Random goals, no matter how well intentioned, are not going to assist you in achieving your vision for your business and your life. Instead, your goals for your business and your life need to be intentional and aligned. Think about any trip you take. The map tells you how to get there but you also see signs along the way that can distract you. Staying connected with the map can keep you on track and allow you to reach your destination.

With that in mind, let's revisit your vision for your future. While it does involve your business, that clearly is not the only thing that your vision includes. Do your current goals for your business align with that vision?

Truthfully, what can happen is that the goals for the business end up being at cross purposes with the goals for the rest of your life. The best way to run a successful business is make sure that it aligns with your purpose and the overall plan for your life.

Sometimes the plan for our lives can appear to be derailed but, ultimately, that detour can lead to big things.

The founder of the unique corporate yoga start-up, Yogist, didn't start out with a plan to open this company. In fact, Anne-Charlotte Vuccino graduated from the HEC Paris and the Copenhagen Business School and had a different career path in mind. Then on a volunteer trip to Benin as a HEC student, she was severely injured in a motorcycle accident. While she was rehabilitating, Vuccino discovered yoga. After getting her master's degree, she began working as a consultant. Her consultant work showed how much stress corporate workers were under, inspiring her to quit her job and start teaching yoga. Today, she brings those benefits to members of the business world. The path to get to where she is today did not follow a straight line, but it aligns her professional and personal paths.

Perhaps you find yourself facing a challenge that has caused you to rethink what you want to do professionally, and it caused you to pick the path of caring for animals. Whatever the reason, remember that what you are trying to do with your business needs to allow you to reach your other goals and dreams. Otherwise, you will find yourself struggling to stay excited and motivated within your business.

With that in mind, let's talk about practical steps you can take when your business is struggling, or you find yourself needing a boost of motivation.

Chapter 7

Running a Business in Challenging Times

While the initial excitement of climbing a mountain keeps you moving forward, the truth is that, over time, the climb itself begins to wear on you. My fellow climbers were also dealing with the physical demands on their bodies and, in some cases, they were too sick to continue.

What kept them motivated was a combination of determination, inspiration, and a willingness to stick with it, even when the path was challenging. The world of business is also like that climb. There are going to be periods of time when you are feeling worn out and frustrated. At that point, you need to make the decision to keep moving forward.

Still, it requires more than just saying to yourself, "I am going to keep at it." During these times, you need a path forward, a plan that will get you motivated through the difficult times you are facing. Another aspect of planning is understanding ways to come up with solutions when faced with the unexpected.

Define the Problem or the Damage

Facing challenges within your business will not always be easy. Learning to face and overcome the challenges without compromising your professional long-term goals is a critical part of being a business owner.

If you are a planner, the unexpected curve ball can be difficult to manage because it is not something that you accounted for in your business plan. That doesn't mean you can't handle the unexpected, but it does mean that you will need to be more flexible than you may have been in the past.

The first thing that you need to do is determine the significance of the challenge by analyzing its degree of impact on your current operations. For instance, during the COVID-19 pandemic, businesses were impacted to varying degrees, depending on the type of business and the local regulations that were in place.

Staying in business meant being creative with how you managed transactions with your customers. Some pet grooming businesses minimized the amount of interaction they had with their customers, picking up dogs outside and instituting online payment systems. However, before they put any of this in place, those owners had to define the problems they faced and how long the situation was likely to stay that way.

Once you have a handle on the circumstances your business is facing, defining your next course of action or the decisions in front of you is easier to determine. Start with small questions and then work out from there. It might be that you have built up the impact of the problem to be more than it actually is. Regardless, defining the problem gives you a place to start as you determine the next steps, instead of just trying to come up with solutions that might not really address the problem at all.

Controlling Your Response

This business is your baby, something that you have invested your heart and soul into. You have given up time and energy, not to mention the financial investment. When you are facing a challenge or problem, it is hard to not get emotional about what it could mean for your business, your team, and your clients.

Once you define the problem, there is likely to be some emotion attached, especially if the impact of the problem could mean having to scale back services or give up progress that you have made in building up your business.

However, if you want to find an effective, logical solution to the problem you face, you can't let your emotions overtake the logical parts of your mind. You need a neutral and steady emotional state in order to find the right solution for your business. That means having strategies in place to help you manage your emotions and stress level.

One of the biggest issues that you will face in controlling your emotional response is that your self-talk can become negative, making it easier for you to tailspin down into the worst-case scenario and focus on the worst. Don't allow negative thoughts to fuel panicked thinking and biased views about what your business is facing.

For bonuses go to ...

Instead of allowing that negativity to take over, focus on the objective aspects of the problem and stay clear on your current reality. Do not allow your imagination to turn you onto a negative line of thought. That could lead you to make less desirable decisions, with larger consequences for your team.

Focus on Your Long-Term Business Goals

When you are facing a problem or a major shift in the market, you might be tempted to make a quick decision. Short-term thinking can lead to impulsive decisions that could end up making the decision even worse.

Instead, focus on your long-term goals and prioritize the needs of the current situation in terms of those goals. Doing so can help you to objectively distance yourself from the problem. It can be so difficult to do that initially.

Short-term problems can feel overwhelming. By keeping focused on the long-term goals, it allows you to see past the things that could be overwhelming and concentrate on being innovative to address the current problems facing your business.

For example, you might have a groomer quit and your next week is completely booked. Instead of focusing on how this could end up costing you clients, it is better to analyze the problem and look for solutions that address the short-term problem.

That could mean calling clients and rescheduling them or asking your groomers to each take on a few extra clients. Instead of focusing on what isn't going right, you are creating plan to move forward and address the short-term problem.

Communicate the Challenge to Your Team

After defining and analyzing the situation, you need to make sure your team understands what is going on. Work with them to implement any steps you might have outlined to deal with the immediate concerns. Be clear about the fact that these steps are a temporary stop-gap measure while you work on a broader solution.

For instance, with the situation of your groomer quitting, the long-term solution is to find and hire another groomer. That takes time, so you need to communicate with your team regarding changes in the schedule and perhaps a temporary limiting of days off to make sure that all the clients are taken care of, or hiring a bather to help assist the groomers with their dogs, which will help minimize their workload as well. The more upfront and transparent you are about the situation, the easier it will be to get your team on board.

When they see you tackling the problem in a calm, informed, and objective way, your team will be more interested in helping you to find a solution that will be a better fit for the long term. Plus, they will be willing to support your efforts to address the situation, because your team will see the benefit to them as well.

For bonuses go to ...

Communication is critical at all stages of your business, because keeping your team informed builds a culture of trust that makes it easier for your team to continue functioning efficiently, while also supporting growth.

Collaborate on a Solution

As business owners, it can be easier to unilaterally come up with the solution or path forward when facing challenges. However, that also means that we are making those decisions with a narrow focus. Other potential solutions can be missed, simply because we are in the mode of putting out fires. When you take the time to collaborate on a solution with your team, you aren't just dealing with the immediate problem, but also learning how to address the problem more efficiently in the future.

While final decision-making will remain with you as the owner and leader, hearing from your team can give you much greater insight into what caused the problem in the first place, and how various solutions might solve the original problem but lead to more challenges. Potential solutions can end up causing additional issues if you are not willing to walk through the solution's long-term impact.

Coming up with two or three different options can help you to weigh the pros and cons, before you settle on the solution with the most advantages. That might not always be easy, so hearing from your team can be a way to uncover advantages that you might not have noticed in the past.

Part of the reason behind collaboration is that you get the benefits of different viewpoints and experiences. It is amazing what your team can come up with as they brainstorm ideas, which can give you more options to choose from before you make your final decision regarding what you move forward with implementing.

At the same time, you might find a solution that addresses the problem right now, but do not assume that the stop-gap measure is a permanent solution. Collaborating with your team can help you to address the current problem, dealing with the challenge while also coming up with some long-term options.

For instance, perhaps you have an issue with scheduling and end up with several clients booked into the same time. The short-term solution might be to offer a discount for the client to reschedule, but you don't want to have to do that on a regular basis.

The goal is to collaborate with your team after the day is done, so you can come up with a long-term solution that will help you avoid overscheduling in the future. It means implementing a specific program that will alert you regarding how many clients are already booked for the day before you book any additional appointments.

Are You Aware of the Situation?

When it comes to building a quality team that will be the backbone of your business, communication is key. That communication needs to flow both ways, down from management and up from your team members.

For bonuses go to ...

Time after time, when workers who left a job are surveyed, they point out how a toxic work environment and poor management played a part in their willingness to quit.

Since your team is likely to be a small one, open communication can help you to head off issues that could fester and lead to team members deciding to quit. After all, it costs a significant amount for you to recruit and hire new employees. Plus, your team is building connections with their clients, so you want to head off any issues to avoid losing both the team member and any clients that prefer to stick with them.

Not only does this involve a high level of communication, but it also requires situational awareness. Be aware of what your employees are dealing with on a daily basis. Doing so can help you to avoid placing demands on them that increase their stress level but not their productivity.

Our business involves employees being able to connect with the clients and their pets. When stress levels are high, that is something those pets can sense, which can end up making the job more difficult.

Yet, when you are situationally aware, you can avoid adding to your team's stress levels and even identify ways to reduce that stress. For instance, how is the overall flow of your shop? Does it make checking pets in easy, and is there a clear path from the wash station to the dryer and then to the grooming stations? If not, the grooming process can become more complicated.

Part of the reason I bring this up is because not every owner is going to be handling pets. Yet, even if you are not a part of the grooming team, you should still be familiar with how the process works and what can be done to make it more efficient for everyone.

Doing so can also lead to greater job satisfaction and better relationships within the workplace. The goal for your business is to grow your client list and make your business profitable.

Our business model means that growth needs to translate into profitability for your team as well. That profitability could mean including incentives based upon their performance. Work on ways to reward your team for providing amazing service to your clients. Doing so can help them to get behind the goals you have for the business, because they feel invested in the outcomes. Plus, it also makes it easier to keep your team solution-focused, because they know that focusing on solutions can benefit them in the long run.

Ultimately, all of the things discussed within this chapter are focused on how you can plan for different challenges, or address them once they present themselves. When you align your business goals and your team, it becomes easier to find solutions to problems and to reach your goals.

Now, let's shift gears away from addressing challenges and the unexpected in your business to another major aspect of the lifecycle of your business. That is when you are ready to move away from running a business and into retirement.

Chapter 8

You Reached the Summit – Now What?

Reaching the top of any mountain is extremely satisfying, but I know that once I reached the top, I was more focused on getting back down. It wasn't until later that I was able to truly process the experience, including how I felt on top of that mountain, looking out at that corner of the world.

When it comes to your business, you may reach a point where you have reached the summit and are now ready to move on to the next adventure. For me, the next adventure was another mountain and opening a business of my own. Now it is writing books and sharing my experiences as an entrepreneur with others looking to start a business in the world of pet grooming. I have shifted into a new niche.

Planning for the Future by Defining Your Niche

The truth is that this business can be profitable, but much of that is based on how quickly you can grow your customer base, and the level of competition in your local market. When you set your prices, they need to be realistic to cover your overhead and keep your business profitable. There are a variety of overhead costs that will be unique to your local market, such as rent and employee wages. How you handle those differences can be the difference between a successful business and one that fails quickly.

As I mentioned before, one of the ways to stand out from the local competition is to offer something slightly different. For instance, can you specialize in working with older pets or those with high anxiety? By specializing, word of mouth about your business will spread among individuals who own those types of pets.

Like anything else, groups of pet owners are gravitating to social media platforms, where they share recommendations about their pet groomers. You can be part of those discussions by searching out those groups and sharing what you offer. It can be a great way to build your clientele even faster than more traditional marketing plans. It is all about finding ways to be different from the other pet grooming businesses in your area.

Another point that makes you stand out is the personal touch you bring to the services that you provide. Not only can you connect with the pets, but you can build a relationship with your clients through their pets. This would allow you to align with your passions and build a future that fits what you want from your life.

Note that in defining how you stand out from the competition, you can also provide a new way to explore your passion for working with pets. This can be helpful when you are ready for the next stage, which could involve stepping away from your business.

If you have owned your business for a long time, you have likely achieved many of your goals, both professionally, personally, and financially. Now you might be looking to the future, trying to determine the next step for your life. Like coming back down the mountain, you need a plan that will ensure that you can safely exit from your business without losing financially or professionally.

With that in mind, let's talk about exit strategies and what they can look like for your business. Although you might not be ready to exit from your business, it is still important to explore exit strategies and include them in your business plan right from the start. You can always revisit these exit strategies as your business grows, making sure that they are still in alignment with your long-term goals.

Making the Decision to Exit

When I purchased my business, the previous owner was ready to move on and do something different. It allowed me to purchase equipment and to grow a business that already had some roots in the community. Of course, as my business grew, I came to the realization that I wanted to teach others how to succeed in this industry.

That meant moving out of the day-to-day operations of my business and turning them over to someone I trusted. It was an exit, but not one that I had planned for. Instead, my husband stepped into the business, and I gradually withdrew from its operations.

For bonuses go to ...

Perhaps you have reached a point where you feel called to do something else, but you don't have a ready successor available. It can feel frustrating if you are essentially stuck in one place without a plan to move forward. Coming up with an exit strategy is about creating that plan and defining what you want to achieve as you leave your business behind and move into your new future.

Fundamentally, a business exit strategy involves planning what will happen as you leave your business. It is a transition, and so your strategy needs to reflect the steps that will trigger the transition, as well as how it will play out. Your business plan served to guide your company throughout its life, and your exit strategy will serve the same purpose.

To be clear, your exit strategy does not mean that your business is in danger of failing, or that a disaster has occurred. In fact, your exit strategy should be a part of your business plan because you will want to move on at some point. Your life has likely been dictated by the needs of starting and maintaining your business, but that doesn't mean you will have the same level of commitment in 5, 10, or 15 years. New opportunities present themselves regularly and that means that, at any given point, you might decide to that it is time for a change.

Defining how the business will transition when you are ready to move to the next phase of your life is a critical part of your exit strategy. To be clear, exit strategies might have multiple aspects, including if your business might meet specific financial goals that trigger the exit plan, or you might reach the point where you are ready to retire.

Regardless of the reason that triggers the exit strategy, you need to consider how you are leaving as well other factors, such as:

- Will you make money on your exit?
- What will happen to the business after you leave?
- Will it continue under new ownership?
- How long will your exit take and what kind of transition period will be necessary?

Keep in mind that as you transition out of your business, either by selling it, passing it on to the next generation, or closing it, your employees are going to be impacted. So, your exit strategy needs to include how the employees will be handled as part of the transition. Your employees are a significant asset, and add value to your business.

As I moved into teaching that helps others to learn how to run a pet grooming business of their own, my husband stepped in and took over much of the day-to-day administration of our pet grooming business. We now have a manager, and will always have one going forward. It provided consistency for our clients and employees because he was familiar with the business and how we operate it.

The point is that we focused on transitioning our business in a way that was beneficial to our family and our employees.

For bonuses go to ...

What Exit Strategy Works for You?

There are several different exit strategies, and each of them has its own pros and cons. When you read through them, think about each of them in terms of your goals and what you want for your future. That framework can help you to determine the best steps to incorporate in your exit strategy.

Continuing the Family Business

Starting a business was a dream come true for you, but when you are ready to move on from the business, you might prefer that your family continue to benefit from what you created. With that in mind, you can create an exit plan that allows for the business to transition to a child or another relative.

The positive is that you can groom your successor, allowing them to work in all aspects of the business and grow their understanding of every process. Keep in mind, though, that this doesn't mean that just anyone in the family is going to be a natural fit for the next stage of the business. By knowing the strengths of the possible successors, you can determine who is likely to be the right fit.

Recognize that this transition might also have a few bumps in the road, especially if you are still involved in the business to some degree. Make sure that your successor doesn't feel undermined by your presence, and give them decision-making power. Doing so will also make it less confusing for your employees as they transition to the new leadership.

On the other hand, you might not be able to find a family member who wants to be part of the business. Even if you have a willing family member, that doesn't necessarily mean that they have the skills necessary to run the business. It can be an emotional and stressful process on family relationships. Plus, partners or investors might also not support your choice of successor, making it more challenging for them to successfully make the transition.

As you can see, there are many positives to being able to transition the business to a family member, but that might not always be possible for a variety of reasons. Make sure that if this is your exit strategy, you are clear about what the transition will look like and what you expect from your family during the process.

Merge With Another Business

Mergers or acquisition as an exit strategy can be a viable option that allows you to hand your business over to someone who is familiar with the industry and customer base, while allowing you to leave with a nice return on your investment into your business.

Depending on who you choose to merge with or sell your business to, you can have the freedom to walk away, or you can continue to have some involvement in the business, although this can be flexible based on how fast you want to transition out of the business.

The best aspect of this strategy is that you can negotiate the price of the sale, which means you can align the price based on the value in terms of assets and your client list. Recognize that, once your business is merged or purchased, it may not operate the same or even maintain any of the aspects of your branding. That can make this strategy emotionally difficult, especially if you have invested in this business and built it from the ground up. Another challenge is that there are a lot of pet grooming businesses, and not everyone is interested in expanding by purchasing someone else's business.

With that in mind, make sure that your exit strategy has a backup plan, in case you are unable to find someone willing to merge with your business or purchase it outright.

Be Part of the Acquihire

Much of the value of your business comes from the people who work with you. After all, clients become attached to specific groomers because of how their pets are handled, and the consistency of the overall look once the grooming has been completed. So don't be surprised if another business wants to buy not your business, but the talent within your business.

If you are looking for an exit strategy that takes away the pressure that comes with being an owner, this solution can allow you to be part of the talent that moves to the new company. You end up negotiating some profit and a successful future for your employees. Plus, if you want to go with them, you can also negotiate your salary without the obligations or responsibilities that come with ownership.

The challenge is that you might not be able to find a business that wants to hire all your employees for the price you hope to get. This situation also means that your business essentially ceases to exist, which can be difficult if you were looking to build a legacy.

Management or Employee Buyout

If family isn't interested in running the business, you might find that an employee or one of your managers is interested in purchasing your pet grooming business. To be clear, this might not be something you can do a lot of advanced planning about, but you can have an idea of how you would like to structure this deal if it were to occur.

The benefit is that an employee or manager is already familiar with the business, ensuring that your legacy will continue. Plus, it will be a smoother transition for both your employees and your clients. There is also the opportunity to stay involved in the business as an advisor or mentor, thus helping them transition from an employee into the ownership role.

You might also be able to structure the sale so that you receive payments over time, allowing for a steady income stream over several years as you transition to a new career or retirement. An employee buyout option can also generate more loyalty among your employees, because they want to see the business be successful not only in the present but the future where they own it.

The challenge is that management transitions can be difficult to implement regardless of who is buying the business, and there is no guarantee that the clients or employees will remain once you are no longer the owner. This could make it less appealing for an employee to be a potential buyer.

That being said, if you want to use this as an exit strategy, consider the employees that might be interested and give them opportunities to learn more about the business before they make a decision. What they learn as you mentor them could also help make the transition easier.

Sell to Your Partner

Depending how your business was structured, you might have a partner who would be interested in buying you out of the business at some point. You could then easily sell off your stake, allowing the business to continue relatively unchanged, while you walk away with a predetermined sale price.

The nice part is that transitioning out of the business will be easier to accomplish without worrying that your clients or employees will be uncared for. Plus, you are dealing with a buyer you already know, and one who is already invested in the business.

The challenge is that if both you and your partner want to sell out at the same time, you may need another exit strategy that allows you both to depart the business. Additionally, you might find it more difficult to maintain any type of role in the business.

Close the Business

Finally, you do have the option to simply close the business and sell off any assets. Your employees would need to find new jobs, because the business would no longer exist. That being said, you might find that it does not result in a significant profit for you, yet it is a way to exit the business if you are ready to go and no buyer materializes.

Closing might also be the only option when you are faced with financial changes that signal the end of the lifecycle of your business. While it is not the end of the world, it can be difficult to face, especially if that means you are essentially having to start over. Regardless of what you face during the many phases of your business, your business plan can include guidelines for executing your transition out.

When crafting an exit strategy, it might be worth exploring what several options look like and incorporating those guidelines into your business plan, thus preparing for various contingencies. The beauty of a pet grooming business is that it provides multiple exit opportunities, allowing you to transition out of your bu

With that in mind, let's talk about what it means when you finally want to exit your business, and how you can move into the next stage of your life, defining the goals that will help you bring your vision to fruition.

Chapter 9

Building on Your Passion for Pets

Climbing a mountain is an invigorating experience. My climbs helped to stretch me mentally and physically, because I accomplished something that was far outside of my experience to that point. Looking back in my journals, I was amazed at my determination to keep going, even as it got physically harder.

Another aspect that I truly enjoyed was learning more about the different cultures, especially when I was climbing in Peru. For instance, in Peru, we were able to learn how they made bricks to build the average home. First, they mix sand and other materials together, smashing it with their feet before putting it into a mold. Once they started to dry, they are removed from the mold and set in the sun to dry on all sides. That can take roughly a week. It takes patience and time to complete all 4,000 bricks for an average home. Yet the results are worth it for the family that occupies that home.

Think about building your pet grooming business. It also took time and patience to reach the point where it was successful, but that time is worth the effort. Recognize that even when things are not going well with your business, it doesn't mean that you aren't learning and growing as an entrepreneur and business owner.

For bonuses go to ...

Even before you start your business, you are gaining skills and knowledge that will benefit your professional goals. What you have already learned can help contribute to the foundation of your business, particularly as you start out at basecamp.

Still, the best way to maximize your potential as a business owner is to connect with mentors and coaches. Let's define the benefits of coaching as you prepare to exit from your business, or during the startup phase.

The Benefits of Coaching

Every mountain that I climbed introduced me to a different set of challenges, forcing me to learn more about myself in the process. It meant understanding that I could do anything I was determined to accomplish. No matter the obstacles in front of me, it was possible for me to achieve my dreams. As my dream evolved, I was able to make moves to bring it to life because I had confidence in my ability, a confidence that grew with every achievement and success. Whether you are ready to open your own grooming business or are ready to sell and move to a new stage of life, confidence will help you to keep moving forward, both in setting and achieving your goals.

Perhaps you are feeling confident about your ability to start this business, and you already have your target market in mind. In order to be successful, I want to make sure that you have all the tools and knowledge necessary. I believe that means recognizing you don't know what you don't know.

Coaching is a way to gain the knowledge you need, while benefiting from the years of experience they your coach has obtained within the industry. I encourage you to reach out and look for a coach or mentor who is familiar with the startup phase of a business, but also this specific industry. If you are looking to exit from your pet grooming business, consider a coach who understands the intricacies of selling your business or transitioning it to the next generation.

Mountain guides were my coaches, teaching and encouraging me throughout the climb. By connecting with coaches and looking for individuals that can serve as mentors, you will obtain both knowledge and encouragement. With the right coaching in place, you can reach your goals and achieve the vision you have for your life and your business, regardless of what stage your business is at.

Eventually, when you reach the summit, there will be a moment when you enjoy the results of all your hard work. But after that, you naturally start looking for the next challenge. In Peru, we had several smaller climbs before we reached the final summit. Yet, as each climb was completed, I couldn't help but look forward to the next climb.

Today, moving out of being part of the daily administration of my company is a leap into the unknown. Yet, I also find myself excited to discover how my experiences and knowledge can benefit individuals who are looking to join this incredible industry.

In Bolivia, there is a bike trail known as the Death Road. It has no guard rails, and the frequent rain and fog often causes limited visibility for those traveling on this road. This infamous road is a narrow dirt road carved right into the side of a mountain. The descent is so rapid that riders feel as if they are being hurled down the side of the mountain. Looking over the side is not for the faint of heart, because it is a 2,000-foot drop!

When you are ready to move on from your business, it can feel like you are hurling down the side of a steep mountain, unsure about what will happen next. You are giving up the comfort and predictability that comes with owning your business and being in charge.

Taking that step into the unknown is not easy, but it is necessary. The transition may be full of holes and unexpected obstacles, but there are also going to be moments of incredible beauty and grace. Those are the moments that will stick with you and motivate you to keep going in the unfamiliar world of life after your business.

While the foundation of any business is roughly the same, pet grooming businesses are unique in terms of what they offer to their clients. We create a family atmosphere, connecting with our clients because we both share a love for their pets. Part of building our business involves creating the right team by hiring the right people.

Now that you are ready to move on to another challenge, you want to make sure that your clients and your team will be well cared for. I was able to transition my business to my husband, someone who understood it and could continue to maintain the high quality of service that I had offered for years to my clients and their pets.

As you create your exit strategy, think about what you want to see happen for your clientele and your team. If your goal is to sell your business to someone who will maintain the business and keep your team, then part of your exit strategy might include looking at some of your current employees as potential owners, or even a way to transition out of the daily operations while still maintaining a level of ownership, as I mentioned in chapter 8.

Recognize that any exit strategy requires specific triggers that will move you to initiate that strategy. For instance, you might not be willing to sell the business until it reaches a specific amount of revenue, making it more valuable to a potential buyer. Once you reach that revenue point, you will want to initiate the process of finding a buyer.

Being up to date on your finances is critical to making sure that any exit happens smoothly, because if you have a strong sense of the expenses and assets, you will be able to negotiate an offer that aligns with the real value of your business.

As you can see, the process of exiting from your business does not need to be something that is conceived last minute, leaving you feeling rushed and struggling to find a buyer. Instead, your exit strategy is all about finding the best way to leave your business, meets your goals and also addresses any concerns that you might have for your clientele and your staff.

For bonuses go to ...

Beyond the Exit

Now, let's talk about what happens after the transition is over. The first morning, you might start out excited to sleep in, but that quickly becomes old. If your exit strategy was not retirement, as is the case for me, you need to figure out what the next step is going to be. You might want to pursue a new career in the same industry, or one in a completely different industry.

Start by spending time envisioning your future. Be descriptive. It might include starting a different business, one that stays in the pet grooming industry but moves away from a traditional sticks and bricks location.

For instance, mobile pet grooming has increased in popularity. Essentially, you are providing door-to-door salon services, including flea and tick baths or basic grooming. The biggest upside for this type of business is that you aren't paying rent or utilities, which means you are reducing your overhead costs. Plus, it can be a real selling point to your clientele that you come to them, instead of them having to pack up their pets and take them to a traditional grooming location.

Notice that you can take your business in a new direction and create a level of flexibility that allows you to do what you enjoy, while still changing up the pace and demands on your time. Whatever you decide to do next, you want to make those decisions with direction, making strategic decisions that help you progress toward your goals.

My exit from my business meant transitioning into the role of coach and teacher. I recognize how these types of businesses can thrive in communities, particularly where people are looking for a high-quality service for their pets. Although there are start-up costs, I also recognized that opening a pet grooming business can be more achievable when you have the knowledge about the industry and its target customers.

By coaching and educating other entrepreneurs, I am giving them the advantage of my years of knowledge and experience to create a solid foundation for their business, while also giving them the tools to grow over time. Eventually, when you are ready to leave your business, you can work with your coach to clearly define what you want for the next phase of your life.

Plus, if you want to remain actively involved in the world of pets, you can create an exit strategy that is right for both your business and your personal goals, thus avoiding unwanted financial consequences for your team after you leave.

You need to define an exit strategy that allows you to let go of managing and running a business, so you can explore other passions and enter the next stage of your life. Our lives are not static, but they are constantly evolving and challenging us to evolve too.

One of the ways to do that is to clearly define what your other passions are. After all, leaving your business might be exciting because it is a chance for you to have more time for exploring your other passions or interests. If you are passionate about pet care, are there other ways that you can be active in that world without running a business, thus enjoying a level of flexibility within your schedule?

Some of these ways can involve volunteering at a local shelter, working for another grooming organization, or even fostering pets before they are adopted by loving families. Understanding what your passions are can be a way to help you define more clearly what you want in the next stage beyond your business.

I have found that moving to coaching allows me to remain active in an industry that I am passionate about, while still providing the opportunity and flexibility to pursue other passions. When you exit from your business, there needs to be a focus on aligning your life around what you want to spend your time doing, not focusing on getting another job or diving right into a new career.

On the other hand, you might find that you enjoyed the process of starting and building a business, but once it matures, you want to exit and move on to the next startup. If that is what you are passionate about, you need to think about the next industry you want to move into, or if you want to move into a different area of the pet industry, as I mentioned earlier.

Therefore, taking time for yourself can be a critical part of the transition process once your exit takes place. It can help you to understand what the best path is for you as you head toward your next summit. Once you reach the top of one mountain, you will be inspired to look for another mountain to climb.

While you should have a business plan that includes an exit strategy for your business, you also need to make sure that you are putting a personal exit strategy in place to allow you to move on to the next stage.

Now, let's talk about how you can incorporate coaching into each stage of your business, and how what you learn during coaching can play a part in your personal life as well.

Throughout each of my mountain-climbing journeys, I grew in my understanding of what it takes to reach a goal. Time and again, I saw the benefits of being determined and sticking with the process, even when there were challenges and obstacles. Those same skills can easily translate into running your pet grooming business.

I want to clear that running a business comes with its own unique set of challenges, but you can successfully deal with them to build a thriving pet business. When I set out to write this book, my focus was on the challenges I faced, and giving you tips that can assist you in planning for similar challenges. But beyond that, I want you to get excited about the possibilities for your personal and professional life.

Think about all the ways that you can contribute to your community as a successful business owner. Not only do you provide a service for pet owners, but you have the opportunity to give back by being active in different events.

For instance, working with a local animal shelter can be a great way to get your name out to new pet parents, while also contributing to the shelter's mission. You might also volunteer to do nail trims at a local adoption event for a rescue. The point is that by connecting with the local pet adoption community, you can get to know the people who are your target customers.

Another wonderful benefit of being a business owner is that you can create a work-life balance to fit your changing needs. In my family, for instance, the change to teaching and coaching individuals to be successful in this industry meant that I needed to shift how I ran my own grooming business. It was that flexibility that really made it work for my family as we shifted priorities.

Chapter 10

Start Climbing to Your Summit!

Perhaps you too are looking for a way to balance your home and family life. By choosing specific days and times for grooming appointments, you can create a schedule that works for your family's life. That being said, when you are building your business, the ideal level of flexibility might not be as readily available. Know that as you build your clientele, you can also build in a measure of flexibility for the other areas of your life.

I find that many new business owners start their business with the dream of working when they want, but the truth is that, in the early days, you are working every day, grooming, marketing your business, handling administrative tasks, cleaning, ordering supplies, booking clients, and so much more. As the business grows, you can delegate some of these tasks, but never underestimate how much time you will initially invest in building your business.

So, what does it take to build a successful business? Let's talk about some of the lessons that I have learned over the years and how you can incorporate them into your pet grooming business.

For bonuses go to ...

Lessons from a Pet Groomer

First, to build a successful business, you need to get your name out there to potential clients. That means using a variety of methods at your disposal. I was creative, using coffee orders to get the name of my business out there. Social media also provides a variety of ways for you to connect with your target clientele. Let's face it, who does not love those pet videos with dogs and cats? As a pet groomer, you can create content or posts that connect with these audiences and allow them to get familiar with your business. But there is more to an online marketing campaign than simply sharing interesting pet posts.

Think about all the different groups online, for every topic under the sun. Pet lovers all have groups, some based on the types of dogs they own, breeders, pet adoptions, special needs dogs and cats, pet care, what to feed your pet, and the list goes on and on. Starting a new pet grooming business means finding ways to connect with these groups, highlighting your expertise and your specialties. With a little creativity, connections can be made that will help your business grow. You can become the go-to expert, which will also help to expand your business.

As I mentioned earlier, if you enjoy volunteering and being active in the community, there are natural ways to pair your community efforts with your business. There are often plenty of methods that allow you to connect with pet parents and show them what you offer. Getting creative can help you in building relationships that turn potential clients into long-term clients that you see regularly.

The focus here is about finding ways to connect with your potential clients. They might be a bit unconventional, but the truth is that your marketing strategy needs to be focused on finding where these potential clients are and then making sure that your brand and your messaging are there too.

Secondly, you want to be sure that you have counted the costs. Even with the best planning, there will be unexpected expenses that come with building out a space for your business. These build-out costs will also depend upon how you want to conduct business. After all, if you want a stationary business, you will have costs related to plumbing, room divisions, creating a drying room, and a retail center.

On the other hand, you might enjoy the flexibility that comes with providing a mobile service to your clients. If that is the case, you will be building out a mobile van or truck with a washing tub, drying area, and grooming table. Your mobile unit will also require being outfitted with water tanks and the proper electrical wiring and panels. Recognize that with a mobile setting, you need ways to refill your water tanks, as well as a pretty good idea of how many pets you can groom with each full tank of water.

As you can see, the best way to control costs is to plan out exactly what type of offerings you want to have, and how you want to serve your clientele. The beauty of this business is that it can be flexible to reach a broader number of individuals, depending on how you want to work.

For bonuses go to ...

When I teach others about building a pet grooming business, I make sure that they spend time thinking about how they want to work, and what type of services they anticipate offering. Too often, I have found that those who build out a space are not doing so with a defined plan, and that can cost them, especially due to unexpected expenses that come from having to make changes to meet building codes or licensing restrictions.

Remember, too, that budgeting for costs is not just about paying for the labor and construction materials. It is also about the permits, inspections, and other licensing that you need to run a business in your area. Before you dive into signing a lease, make sure that the space can be converted properly.

Not only does the space need to be in a commercial zoned area, but it also needs to have enough space for you to define the different areas clearly, and have space for multiple pets. If it is not zoned properly, you could put out funds with no return. Since starting a new business is already an expensive venture, having to pay for a lease on a space that won't work for your business can quickly eat into your investment capital.

Additionally, retail is something to consider. Where will you put your inventory? How much inventory do you want to have on hand? Will there be a wide variety of offerings, or just a few specific ones related to the services you offer, such as shampoos for home use, or brushes? These questions can help you clarify how extensive you want this part of your business to be, as well as how much space you need to designate for it.

As you can see, the costs and build-out of a space involve thought and planning about what you want your business to be, and what areas you want to focus on as part of the services and amenities you will be offering to your clients. Once you have defined your business, you are ready to start looking for space, building it out, and getting your new clients in the door.

Reaching the Summit

Here I want to talk about the summit of the mountains from a different point of view. First, building a business from the ground up is like setting up those initial basecamps. Every part of your initial planning should be focused on what you want your business to look like, and the costs involved. However, once those basecamps have been achieved, your focus shifts to further up the mountain.

The climb takes time but every camp you reach means that you have gotten that much closer to achieving your goal. For some of you, the initial summit is actually opening your doors and running a profitable business. As time goes on, the new summit will be growing your clientele to the point that you can afford to expand your team. Other goals might be expanding your retail offerings or providing additional services to draw in different types of clients.

Why do I mention these different goals? Because the best and most successful business owners are not the ones who just focus on running their business daily. The most successful are the ones who set new goals and focus on building and growing their business daily. They

For bonuses go to ...

see a bigger picture of where they want to take their business, and then make decisions to align their business with that larger goal.

Naturally, as you grow your business, you will want to think about ways to manage costs and be proactive during times of inflation or recession. After all, pet owners are using your service because it is convenient and likely fits their budget. However, if things change economically, your clients could also reduce the number of times they bring their pets in for a groom. That could end up leaving you with open appointments and a reduced income to cover overhead expenses.

I believe the best offense is to stay flexible for your current clients and not to stop marketing for new clients. The reality is that economic changes impact households differently. The answer to a reduced number of bookings by your regular clients is to increase the number of clients coming in, even if they only book one or two sessions over the course of several months. You want to keep your calendar full, thus allowing your business to continue to thrive.

Encourage clients to book multiple appointments in advance, and perhaps give a loyalty reward for doing so. Offering online booking to ease the process. It might be a $5 coupon or an upgrade for one of their grooming appointments for free. Remember, the goal is to build good relationships with your clients, so they will talk about you and entice other potential clients to walk in the door.

www.tanyaellis.com

Growth is a Mindset

One of the final points I want to make is that you are the heart of your business. Your decisions, values, and beliefs will be reflected in how your business operates. When you decide that failure is just a learning process, and mirror that mindset for your staff and clients, you allow your business and team to grow and learn from the mistakes that will inevitably occur.

You need to encourage a growth mindset, instead of just focusing on the mistakes and concluding that you can't accomplish what you set out to do. This mindset can inspire your team to continue to learn, which will help your clients to feel more comfortable with leaving their beloved pets with you.

On the mountains I climbed, there were moments when I wondered if I could make it to the top. But I dug down deep, determined to achieve what I set out to do. For example, while hiking the Inca trail at the end of a long 10 hour hike, 6 of those hours were rainy, and at the end of the hike I was so tired that I bumped into a tent pole and almost tumbled over the side of the path where there was a big drop. Someone helped by catching me. I ended up with a huge bruise the size of a cantaloupe on my left side of my thigh. But I got some nice down time and a good night's rest to get ready for the final day. I was willing to learn from the guides that were available. I didn't see myself as a failure because I struggled at different points of the journey. Instead, I saw myself learning and moving forward to achieve my goal of reaching the top.

For bonuses go to ...

For you to run your business and achieve your goals, both the short- and long-term ones, it is critical that you adopt a growth mindset. See yourself being successful, and acknowledge that mistakes do not mean that your goals are unattainable.

Your growth mindset gives you permission to experiment, learning what works for your business, your clients, and your team, as well as what doesn't work for them. You might be surprised at how inspired you can be to keep moving forward because you believe that your efforts will pay off in the long run.

Running a business also means that you have stepped out of the comfort zone of having a traditional paycheck. It means that your energy and investment into your business will not stop when you open the doors. In fact, you will likely be reinvesting profits into your business for a significant period of time.

Part of investing in your business means investing in yourself. Take time to reflect on what might be changing in your community, and how that could impact your business. Reflecting on your business regularly can also help you to see where you might need to make adjustments to your business plan, or even see how some processes might no longer be contributing to your success.

Changes will always be a part of this journey of entrepreneurship, so don't get so emotionally attached to a specific way of doing things that you are unwilling or unable to make changes that will help you to improve. When we don't embrace change as business owners, we can end up impeding our own success.

So even if it is terrifying to take the leap, know that you will benefit from the experience and the knowledge you gain, regardless of the challenges that you might face along the way. Focus on the process, not the results, because that is where you truly gain the most knowledge about what works and what doesn't work for your business.

At the end of the day, you determine what you are capable of, and once you decide that, no one can tell you otherwise. That puts you in the position to successfully complete the climb up any mountain. The goals you set for your business can be large or small, but by taking the leap to open your pet grooming business, you are now one step closer to achieving those goals.

I want you to get excited about this new adventure as a business owner and entrepreneur. Visit me on my website (insert website), where I offer more chances for you to grow your professional network through various educational opportunities. Be a part of this amazing community and see each of your goals as another part of your journey to reach the summit!

About the Author

Tanya Ellis is an entrepreneur, author of *My Passion 4 Business: 10 Steps to Opening a Pet Grooming Salon*, and business coach. Not only does she love pets, but Tanya also provides quality grooming services to other pet owners, giving them peace of mind, knowing their pets are well cared for.

Tanya provides real-world experience and knowledge to those looking to open a pet grooming business. Her focus is on helping them to identify potential pitfalls and plan accordingly.

With over a decade of industry experience, Tanya believes in the importance of being your own boss. She has also climbed mountains around the world, sharing her experiences, and how they can relate to starting and growing a business.

Currently, she lives with her husband and family, along with her own beloved pets, while running her educational and grooming businesses.

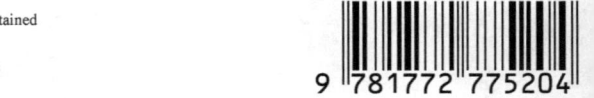